AMERICAN REBOOT

by

Paul Adams

1

AMERICAN REBOOT

Email: erepublic@usa.com

ISBN-13: 978-1722027841

ISBN-10: 1722027843

The Future is Yours

You have an advantage other generations did not have, and the Founding Fathers could only have dreamed of. You have the internet and social media. In minutes a message can spread like wildfire. As more people demand that their input count, a form of direct democracy has been emerging. Questions put to ballot are now put to opinion polls. Like never before, populism is emerging as the next emancipation Wave. First slaves were freed. Now, it's the Truth.

For the first time ever, the People have the ability to arrive at a consensus that can be compared to the hive effect, a collective mind instantly acting in perfect unison. This surge for truth thanks to outlets like WikiLeaks and Project Veritas is your greatest defense in protecting America from Globalists. It will lead to greater transparency, accountability of rogue elements and lesser waste of resources, and fewer wars. The multinational corporations rely on obfuscation to achieve their ends.

If the Globalists shut the internet down, we will have lost the battle. America will be no more. The internet must remain neutral. If it becomes regulated, then it's time to create an alternative internet, as Russia is doing.

We are under siege; time is of the essence. Do your own research if you must, and you will discover that my findings and the solution outlined further down, are seminal.

America is relatively a young nation, a maturing experiment, a work in progress, and like any invention, requires an upgrade every so often. As its rightful owners, you the People, have the innate right and the obligation to diagnose and repair your nation from the foundation up; you must check off the flaws and strengths and make adjustments. Needless to say, there are many faulty faucets. But, the definition of insanity is to keep repeating the same mistakes hoping for success. If only the People are transparent to the Government, the result is tyranny. On the other hand if the Government becomes transparent to the

People, freedom and peace will return and the Constitution will reign supreme as the highest law in the land.

There are, and always will be, masters of the universe (MOTU), who will want to control nations by bribes and blackmail. They hide behind multi-layered curtains while their henchmen and useful idiots do their dirty work. Some of these MOTU include the Ford Foundation, the Carnegie Foundation, the Bush's, the Rockefeller's, the Clinton's, elements in the CIA and the Pentagon, as well as front men like George Soros and Henry Kissinger.

Hillary Clinton referred to the CFR as the 'Mother Ship'. They all have one thing in common: they don't want to be detected by the masses; so they shroud themselves in philanthropy, a bit like the Vatican has a white and black Pope. They have their gatekeepers and controlled opposition.

There will always be others to replace them when they fade away.

As George Soros put it, "I am part of a small group of Extremists". These are the elements that have been working to dissolve the sovereignty of the United States of America over decades. They create distractions to disarm the populace.

Unless you decide to reassert your role as the owners and employers and until your public servants and employees realize they are on the People's payroll, you will only get more of the same. Never forget that. Empowering the People is the only and final solution for the ultimate form of Democracy: an interactive Representative Republic, with teeth.

Never be satisfied with a headline until you have researched it from every possible angle. Who is standing to gain by the story? Who are they trying to manipulate? What kind of mind trap is this? What reaction are they trying to evoke? Who owns the media outlet? What stories has it spewed in the past?

The media is owned by powerful Zionist interest (I am not making any aspersions on Jews – they are a category separate unto themselves). The Federal Reserve is controlled by the wealthiest bloodlines, and Congress is effectively owned by the Zionist Israeli lobby - that uses blackmail as its primary weapon of choice.

As at this printing, by some estimates, 9% of top positions in government are held by Dual-Citizen Israelis. This should make anyone pause and think.

Beware of anyone who points to the banks as the topmost layer. There are forces above the banks. Beware of triple sugar-coated cyanide pills in the form panacea promises. They appear useful on the surface, but contain lethal doses of state-dependency that enrich the few at the top, irrespective of their socialist or capitalist leanings.

The struggle is not between democrats and republicans or between big government and small government.

The struggle is between self-determination and globalism; it's between populism and elitism. On a fundamental level it's a battle between the proponents of free agency and the purveyors of mind-control - because power is the ultimate opium.

It's a struggle between the few at the top who want complete mastery over the world, and the People at the bottom who simply want to live their lives in peace and with purpose and goodwill, but are forever being distracted and divided.

Wars benefit the 1% at the expense of the masses. Never buy into their official story. 9-11 was an inside job, planned long in advance with Mossad fingerprints all over it. To make the point: Larry Silverstein had the blueprints for the new design of the World Trade Center as far back as April 2000, fourteen months before he became a leaseholder of the WTC.

And he announced this in public. Look up a short video on YouTube entitled 'Larry Silverstein Explains 9/11 in 90 seconds.'

If you haven't invested at least 100 hours researching 9-11, in my books, you really don't care about America. If you came back from a vacation and saw your home demolished and the explanation given to you by authorities was that this was the work of termites, how would you respond? It's not a conspiracy to want to investigate a crime scene.

An American reboot requires that you start questioning official narratives; never take anything at face value or you and your children might end up as cannon fodder.

Reserve judgment until you have gathered all the facts. Use alternative news outlets instead of the MSM to arrive at your conclusions. Question everything!

There are counterfeit politicians who start out as loyal nationalists (Trump is a prime example), who will promise you Utopia, but are, in reality, Trojan Horses – and often they don't even know it, until they get into office. The elite will finance politicians of every political stripe to hedge their bets. Think of the forces that can 'JFK' Trump in an instant if he doesn't deliver.

Tell me who is funding a candidate and I'll tell you who will be running the country. Sheldon Aledson funded Trump and the GOP.

Never forget the 2016 Democratic National Convention steal, where Bernie Sanders capitulated after the voting was clearly going in his favor. Few news outlets will tell you that Hillary Clinton stole 13 states during the primaries.

Then, WikiLeaks disclosed corruption by such tools as Debbie Wassermann Schultz, who was immediately hired by the Clinton campaign after she was forced to step down as DNC chair. Hillary had planned a $5 Million extravaganza victory party, replete with celebrities and a glass ceiling, while Newsweek had 165,000 copies of her on the cover as the new President. Trump, was, as Robert David Steele said correctly, the accidental President.

There are other indicators that Trump has been bought by the Israeli lobby. Firing 59 missiles into Syria without an independent fact-finding mission is one such clue.

If the latest blockchain technology is not being used in online voting, and if voter ID and bio-metrics are not integrated in voting stations, election fraud will be forever endemic to the banana republic.

Project Veritas and WikiLeaks have let the genie out of the bottle. There is no going back to business as usual.

The future points to an eRepublic, a government that is truly of, by and for the People, whereby the People, as the owners and keepers of their government can ratify constitutional amendments, vote on Bills and referendums, and, most radically, recall elected officials before their term expires, through a Secured Online Citizen Account. This innovation is well within the proper and necessary clause of the Constitution since it only makes for a more transparent system of checks and balances, the very ideal the Founding Fathers were aiming for.

Congressional Districts will no longer be echo chambers where constituents come to hear their voices bounce off the walls.

America must be rebooted, re-invented, upgraded into a Democracy where the People are the true keepers and stewards of their Republic.

This is why the Globalists are in such a panic mode and will waste no time arguing against such an upgrade. Instead, they will create another crisis to distract the masses.

Beware of headlines that call for knee-jerk reactions. Know your enemy's playbook. Read 'Rules for Radicals' by Saul Alinsky, for a primer on how the enemy operates. Learn about the Hegelian Dialectic. Read 'War is a Racket'. You must think like the enemy if you are going to beat the enemy.

Always shine the light on their lies. Do it forcefully, relentlessly. Give them no quarters. The rats hate it when light shines on them.

From a 30K foot level, history is made by carefully defining your ends at the outset. The ends determine the means. And for the enemies of Free-Will (populism) the end is a Luciferian dystopia.

Each end game will require different modalities. The globalists are ruthless, fierce and unapologetic. Don't expect any remorse or regret from them. They are vampires camouflaging as humanitarians. They make no concessions. They exist only to achieve one thing: their goal; not a compromised middle ground.

This experiment - America - you must upgrade, just like you upgrade your web browser. Make technology your servant.

When people love things more than people, things turn ugly. Take time to connect with the power of love. Only then, will you be able to be transformed. The less your happiness depends on materialism, the more you are. The enemy wants you to believe that the less you own, the less you are. I am writing this after 3 years of living as a nomad. And I've had it all. I've lived in 9 countries, had palatial homes.

There is a time for planting and a time for reaping. It's not so much the destination that counts, as much as the journey.

Political bankruptcy has its roots in moral bankruptcy. If the 'everyone is doing it' excuse is used, there are no limits to the level of depravity a nation can sink into. The planet can only be at peace when the Golden Rule is practiced.

The two-party system is a false illusion of choice intended to divide and conquer. It keeps the masses preoccupied and fighting over issues that cannot be resolved by any party, because both parties are owned by the same powers. Look for a candidate who will empower the people, will uphold the Constitution, and will put American nationalism first.

Promises mean nothing. Politicians will use focus groups, polls, meta-data to determine how to best position their platform. It takes a well-researched sales pitch, packaged and prepared to brand the candidate. Once he is elected, his promises are null and void. He is in Wag the Dog.

This should not be news to anyone. Once again, let me repeat: the only remedy is a reboot!

Wars are horrific and will be even more so in the future. Avoid wars at all costs. Choose people who have fought in wars and know firsthand of their horrors. It is better to be an isolationist than the world's police force. The world's hate for America will only increase the more it tries to appease Israel's appetite for aggression and the more it asserts itself as the world's police force.

Note: wars profit shareholders of weapons manufacturers. Those stock prices must keep going higher. As a former stockbroker, I can guarantee you prices are not meant to go lower.

China seeks to be the next world power. It will back candidates who will create a war in which the USA will lose. Hint: Hillary Clinton wore Mao pant suits.

George W. Bush spilled the beans when he told a reporter that commercial interests sometimes trump national security and peace. 9/11 was an example of that statement put into action.

Most wars are about pillaging a country's resources, replacing its central bank with a Rothschild central bank, arming the new puppet regime, and then deposing it with more wars. If an invading army killed over a 500,000 of our children we would also be mad as hell. It's called Blowback. The globalists love Blowback. They can use that as a pretext to cull our civil rights. War is a win-win for them.

Don't allow the globalist to use America's best and brightest as cannon fodder. Beware of false flags. They are self-inflicted wounds that are made to appear as though whatever flavor of the week enemy has attacked us. Question everything that appears like an attack, and is pushed by the MSM as another terrorist attack.

With every crisis comes the suspension of the Constitution and the invocation of Continuity of Government measures. As things stand currently (2018), Trump approves indefinite detention without due process; he also approves warrant-less searches and spying of Americans, and asset forfeiture.

So much for his oath of office to protect, preserve and defend the Constitution. He is disconnected from the America the Founding Fathers tried so hard to frame.

Keep your minds and bodies unpolluted. The enemy knows that a mind that is obsessed with pornography, for example, or drugs, disconnects from one's higher source that can 'inspire', and with the hive. Trump is the anti-thesis of a clean mind. His actions with women prove it.

When enough people are living clean lives (not perfect lives) the hive will receive communication from Heaven and act as One. America was meant to be a nation under God. Right now its functioning as a nation owned by a foreign-owned central bank, Dual-Citizens of Israel and a Zionist controlled media.

Leaders lead by example. Tyrants lead by duplicity. Even without a President, the People can still manage if they are connected to the source, God. I am afraid they are more likely to be connected to the enemy of God.

Don't underestimate the power of prayer; or the power of spells and hexes by witches and warlocks, either.

The word 'ligament' has its origins in the Latin 'ligare', which means 'to tie' or 'to bind'. The word religion comes from 'religare', which means 'to reconnect' to the source. But once you know how to reconnect, my view is that the religious organizations are as good as school academies. Once you know how to drive, the academy has served its purpose. Time to move on.

Everyone is connected to some intelligent source, whether good or evil. The elite, given their proclivity to depravity and wars, are mostly connected to the forces of deception. What agency's motto is: By Deception Make War?

If we ever forget that we are One Nation Under God, then we will be a nation gone under. ~ Ronald Reagan

When a nation elects the best liars, that nation is politically bankrupt.

Devote some time daily to reflect on the big questions, like: how can I be a little more truthful, kinder, more empathetic today? Never cringe in the face of lies. Expose them, relentlessly, as if your life depended on it! Because it really does.

You Silence denotes Consent to the enemy. It is your silence that is causing the most destruction to your nation. Take ten minutes each day to study the Constitution until you know its critical mass like the back of your hand.

Always remember there have been over 11,500 proposals for amendments since the inception of the Constitution. Only 27 were ratified as amendments, of which 10 are the Bill of Rights. Keep brightly lit in your mind Amendments 9 and 10. They give powers and rights to the People, not listed in the Constitution. It's another of swaying: if this experiment goes south, the People are the final arbiters.

Those who seek to empower the People, to educate the People, to bring comfort to the People will be the People's greatest leaders. They will serve and protect the People as a father does his family.

Just as the household cannot be labeled 'socialist' or 'capitalist', neither should a country have to flail in the wind every four years trying to decide whether to vote conservative or liberal. Pragmatism is required to keep moving forward.

Don't get boxed-in the false divide-and-conquer, liberal v conservative construct. Vote for people with character.

Questions relating to life and death, and rights and privileges of minorities are better resolved through plebiscites, not the Supreme Court which has been known to be an appendage of the political apparatus.

Abortion and gay rights issues cannot be adjudicated by left-leaning or right-leaning Supreme Court justices. Only the people can decide in matters (Res) that pertain to the public (Publica). Don't let Hollywood decide on matters that will resonate through eternity.

Political parties will create economic hardship in order to be elected into power and provide solutions for the masses. Both parties will export job, will create bank implosions that you will be called to bail, both will implement policies that limit the flow of capital to community banks. One party creates problems for the other party to fix in the next election. It's like tag team wrestling. What party has ever lowered the National Debt? That should be your clue.

Expect the new party in power to increase budget deficits and the national debt with more wars, more pilfering, more waste and corruption. All the while, both parties are given marching orders by supranational interests. They are slowly boiling us like the proverbial frog.

In the Iraqi war, over 100,000 private contractors were hired. Who profits in a war? What companies have claims to oil reserves in a foreign nation we are about to attack? Cui bono? This is the first question to ask, before sending troops to war. Ask any defense contractor if war is not good for business.

A party that creates divisiveness is a party that wants to remain in power. It cares only about the wealth of the few at the top. The Republicans are infiltrated by neocons whose objective is to enrich the military-industrial-media complex by creating more wars and destabilization in the middle east. Again, cui bono?

The Democrats are infiltrated by Marxists to the point where universities should be registered as subversion centers. They are funded by big banks and billionaires the likes of George Soros. The elite profit in any economy.

The CFR, the Trilateral Commission, the Bilderbergs, the Vatican (controlled by the P2-Lodge), the Illuminati, The Muslim Brotherhood, CAIR, Russia, The World Zionist Organization, all have moles in the US government.

Beware of government officials with dual citizenship. Beware of the Constitutionalists draped in Americana who are pushing for routine interventionism, and, especially, interventionism on behalf os Israel.

America for many around the world is a fat cow that should be feasted on. Your tax dollars are paying for their meals. Israel, for example, receives $30,000 a year for every man, woman, and child.

The End-Game can be sometimes more metaphysical than geopolitical. The aim for can be a one world government. For others it's an Islamic Caliphate; for still others, it's the Greater Israel Project; or an era where Lucifer reigns in the form of Supreme Leader who will promise Peace, after nations have been exhausted economically, politically, and morally – order out chaos.

The one thing they all have in common is they control US politicians with bribes, blackmail, death threats (to them and their families), and proven intimidation tactics that often lead to mysterious suicides. This has been the devil's modus operandi since the dawn of time.

The prospects for the future may seem hopeless and dire, but there is a solution: an American reboot.

25

It's easy to bribe or blackmail a few hundred people in Congress or even a President, but it's very hard to pull that off on three hundred million people who are in direct control of their government and know who the enemies area.

This is why eDemocracy is having such an impact globally and is the only remedy if America is to surge forward in a new era of peace and prosperity. The solution calls for the inversion of the pyramid; it will place the People, now at the base of the Pyramid at the top and the 1% at the apex at the bottom.

By using the latest blockchain technologies the People can form a government that is truly of, by and for the People. Switzerland is a worthy template. The Swiss must now make voting more people-friendly by taking it online to avoid the long lineups; the Swiss already have one year term limits.

That is the future. Had the Founding Fathers lived in our day, they would have drooled at the technologies we have, such as: polygraphing, polling and the internet.

They would have included provisions in the Constitution that gave the People the greatest control and ownership over their Republic utilizing the latest cutting edge technologies.

The People of the United States will only be able to have a government that is of, by and for the People when corruption has been eliminated and the People are the rightful owners and beneficiaries of their government.

If we reform the House of Representatives, fewer people at the top will be corrupted, and the disconnect between constituents and House Reps will disappear. If agencies are currently polygraphing their government employees, certainly the American people can polygraph their employees. If America is to survive, it must eliminate the corruptible middlemen who claim to represent the people, when in reality they only represent their special interest donors. The People, of this nation, at whose behest the Constitution was drafted, must reboot America. No one else can do it for them; rest assured, the last thing Congress wants is to be held accountable to the People.

We need visionaries in your generation who can foresee hundred of years into the future. The clock is ticking.

Imagine if each US citizen had a Secured Citizen Online Account that accessed their Congressional District, much just like an encrypted online bank account or PayPal account; only with this SCOA you would use bio-metric verification - a retinal and/or fingerprint scan. With such an account the People would be able to vote on Bills and referendums, vote in national and state elections, recall officials at the Executive, Senate, state and local levels, and ratify amendments to their Constitution. How cool would that be!

Would this not be much better than what we have now? The Founding Fathers were radicals. They were inventing a system of government that had never existed before. You, the People, now must pick up from where they left and don't let anyone that it can't be done. It's do or die time.

You will never have walked more proudly as an American than when you will have rebooted America. Guaranteed!

Never be afraid to be a radical, to be innovative, to dare think out of the box. This initiative will require public debate. Spread the word; hold town hall meetings. What do you have to lose? Other than your sovereignty? America has always been about inventing radical solutions - which everyone else copies. Maybe China could copy this.

You will come across gatekeepers, moles and shills, especially if they are big on peripheral issues but neglect the big central make-or-break issues. They will distract you. They will call for a Constitutional Convention to shorten Congressional term limits. A Red Herring! They want the same insanity, only with faster turn-arounds. They offer solutions which do not remedy the problem, but only exacerbate it. There is no end to their sinister tactics.

Ask yourself: why would they employ cops with sketchy backgrounds? These bad cops then give good cops a bad name. What could the system want to introduce? How about a federal police force – perhaps a UN or SS police force?

Can you see how problems are created to install faulty solutions?

The Hegelian dialectic manifests itself in social engineering, false flags, and catastrophes, all created to elicit a reaction from the public. The public will demand solutions and remedies. And the elite will be more than happy to oblige.

When Supreme Court Justices create laws to override plebiscites, the will of the People has been silenced, and the Republic is nothing more than a totalitarian state masquerading as a Republic.

There are many ways for the People to forfeit liberty. You must begin thinking like your enemy to understand their next move. Because there is always going to be another move. What conditions would bring America to its knees and how could that be accomplished? Gun confiscation would be one objective. What next?

I recommend that every American knows how to build an AR15 from an 80% lower receiver. Just buy parts and start building.

What social engineering strategies would have to come into effect in order to accomplish their goal of gun confiscation?

When you see a crisis blow up in the MSM what is the reaction they are trying to evoke? Why, for example, would they want to incite violence during an election? What if they want to collapse the federal government from within by first discrediting the moronic establishment?

What if they are exporting jobs to crank up unemployment, poverty and crime in order to discredit the federal government and point us to the NWO?

What if they contrived the sub-prime housing bubble to create more poverty and disillusionment; blow by blow over decades to pummel the public and bring about the conditions for a massive meltdown after the People have completely lost faith in their government?

What if the balkanization of America is their end game, to turn us into another Iraq?

What if the expansionism, interventionism and nation-building was orchestrated not to spread democracy but to create an intense hate against America, a hate which would trigger terrorism, a clash of civilizations, and eventually a take-down of America?

Are you awake, yet? You need to take the blinders off and smell the coffee! I will finish with some quotes from past Presidents.

I must study politics and war that my sons may have liberty to study mathematics and philosophy. ~ John Adams

In matters of style, swim with the current; in matters of principle, stand like a rock. ~ Thomas Jefferson

Our Constitution was made only for a moral and religious people. It is wholly inadequate to the government of any other. ~ John Adams

Power always thinks... that it is doing God's service when it is violating all his laws. ~ John Adams

Motivation is the art of getting people to do what you want them to do because they want to do it. ~ Dwight D. Eisenhower

We must guard against the acquisition of unwarranted influence, whether sought or unsought, by the military-industrial complex. ~ Dwight D. Eisenhower

Do you want to know who you are? Don't ask. Act! Action will delineate and define you. ~ Thomas Jefferson

Our greatest happiness does not depend on the condition of life in which chance has placed us, but is always the result of a good conscience, good health, occupation, and freedom in all just pursuits. ~ Thomas Jefferson

I know of no safe depository of the ultimate powers of the society but the people themselves; and if we think them not enlightened enough to exercise their control with a wholesome discretion, the remedy is not to take it from them but to inform their discretion. ~ Thomas Jefferson

When there is a lack of honor in government, the morals of the whole people are poisoned. ~ Herbert Hoover

Every government degenerates when trusted to the rulers of the people alone. The people themselves are its only safe depositories. ~ Thomas Jefferson

I have always been afraid of banks.
~ Andrew Jackson

It is neither wealth nor splendor; but tranquility and occupation which give you happiness. ~ Thomas Jefferson

Our government is founded upon the intelligence of the people. I for one do not despair of the republic. I have great confidence in the virtue of the great majority of the people, and I cannot fear the result. ~ Andrew Jackson

It is the youth who must inherit the sorrow, the tribulation... that are the aftermath of war. ~ Herbert Hoover

Few men have virtue to withstand the highest bidder. ~ George Washington

If we ever forget that we are One Nation Under God, then we will be a nation gone under. ~ Ronald Reagan

The basis of our political system is the right of the people to make and to alter their constitutions of government.
~ George Washington

To you Millennials
We hand over
The Torch of Freedom.
Learn from the past or be
Doomed to repeat it.

*If politicians are too corrupt to prosecute
because they will topple the entire
government, then it's time for a reboot.*
~ Paul Adams